Dedication

This devotional is dedicated to every person who has experienced a life-changing moment and may not have had the journey's map to figure it all out.

May God continue to lead and guide us as we be childlike and trust Him wholeheartedly while we take the next step with faith.

How This Book Works

What?! is a 90-day journey divided into three parts:

Part One: Acknowledge (Days 1-30) Before we can move forward, we have to acknowledge where we are. In this section, we name what happened, identify what we're feeling, face our fears, and anchor ourselves in who God is.

Part Two: Attend (Days 31-60) Once we've acknowledged the disruption, we go deeper. We examine what we believed before, what is being uprooted, who is with us, and what God says about our identity.

Part Three: Align (Days 61-90) Finally, we orient ourselves toward what comes next. We discover what is still true, what new thing is possible, who we are becoming, and what fruit we want to cultivate.

WHAT?!

TIANA *TEE* TOWNSEND

A 90-DAY DEVOTIONAL FOR WHEN LIFE CHANGES EVERYTHING

AUTHOR OF

THE JOURNEY TO SELF

AND

A SEAT ON THE COUCH

Copyright

How to Use Each Day

Each daily entry includes:

Scripture:

A verse to anchor the day's reflection.

Reading:

A short devotional thought, often including pieces of my own story.

Sit With This:

Journaling prompts and exercises. This is where the real work happens. Don't rush past these. Grab a pen. Be honest. Let yourself process on the page.

Carry This Forward:

A brief prayer to take into your day.

A Few Suggestions

Go at your own pace: This is a 90-day devotional, but if you need to sit with a day for longer, sit. If you need to skip a day and come back, come back. There's no grade. There's no timeline. There's just you and God doing the work.

Don't skip the writing: The journaling prompts are not optional extras. They are where transformation happens. Something shifts when we move thoughts from our heads onto paper. Give yourself the gift of writing it out.

Find your people: Consider going through this devotional with a friend, a small group, or a therapist. The "Who Is With Me?" section in Part Two will help you identify your community - but don't wait until Day 45 to reach out. You don't have to do this alone

Be gentle with yourself: This book will ask you to sit with hard things. If a day feels too heavy, it's okay to pause. The "If You Are Struggling Today" note at the beginning of this book has resources if you need them.

One More Thing

I'm not writing this from the other side, pretending I have it all figured out. I'm writing this as someone still in process. Still learning to trust. Still taking the next step with faith.

That's all any of us can do.

So let's begin. Whatever your "What?!" moment was, God is not finished with you yet.

He who began a good work in you will carry it on to completion.

Turn the page. Let's go.

- Tiana

Introduction

You picked up this book because something happened.

Maybe it was a phone call that changed everything. A diagnosis. A divorce. A death. A betrayal. A job loss. A move you didn't choose. Or maybe it was something that should have been good news but left you reeling anyway - a promotion, a pregnancy, an opportunity that terrified as much as it excited.
Whatever it was, you found yourself standing in the wreckage of your expectations, asking one question:

What?

I've been there. More than once.
I've stood in my kitchen staring at the trash can, realizing I was now a divorced, non-coparenting single mother who had to figure out everything alone. I've sat through hours-long assessments as my son was diagnosed with level 3 Autism, then driven home wondering how our lives would work. I've driven 500 miles back to a hometown I swore I'd left behind, fleeing trauma I never saw coming, only to discover that God was making a way in what felt like wilderness.

I didn't have a map for any of it. I wished I did.
This devotional is the map I wish I'd had.

A Note

If You Are Struggling Today

This devotional asked you to sit with hard things. That is sacred work, but it is also heavy work. If at any point the weight feels too much to carry, please know this:

It is okay to step back: Putting this book down for a day, a week, or longer is not failure. It is wisdom. You know your capacity better than anyone.

It is okay to ask for help: If you are experiencing thoughts of self-harm, overwhelming hopelessness, or emotional pain that feels unmanageable, please reach out. A trusted friend. A pastor. A counselor. A crisis line.

National Suicide Prevention Lifeline: 988

Crisis Text Line: Text HOME to 741741

You are not meant to carry this alone. God often delivers comfort through the hands and voices of others. Let Him send you help.

You are seen. You are valued. Your life matters. And there is no shame in needing support.

— Tiana

Part One

Acknowledge

Days 1-30

"Be still and know that I am God." — Psalm 46:10

Before we can move forward, we have to acknowledge where we are.

This first part is not about fixing, solving, or finding silver linings. It is about honoring what happened. Naming it. Sitting with it long enough to understand what we are actually carrying.

Over the next thirty days, we will do the sacred work of acknowledgment. We will name what just happened. We will identify what we are feeling—not just the obvious emotions, but the ones hiding underneath. We will face our fears honestly. And we will anchor ourselves in who God is, even when everything else feels uncertain.

You do not have to have it together for this journey. You do not have to perform healing or rush toward resolution. You just have to be here. Present. Honest. Open.

That is enough. You are enough. And God is with you in this.

Let us begin.

Week One

What Just Happened?

Day 1

"The Lord is close to the brokenhearted and saves
those who are crushed in spirit."

Psalm 34:18 (NIV)

I remember standing in my kitchen, looking at the trash can.

It sounds small, I know. But that trash can represented everything. I had spent years building a home with someone. We had created a life together. We had a son together. And now it was just me.

Just me to figure out how to put everything together. Just me to take out the trash—which seems ridiculous to mention, but I am NOT a trash person, and suddenly that was my job too. Just me to protect us. Just me and my one-year-old, figuring out how to survive in a new city and state.

No one else to balance ideas off of when it came to raising my child. No one else to share the weight. Just me, standing in a kitchen tasked to make it feel like home. The only thing that played in my mind is "How did I end up here?" "What just happened?"

Maybe your "What?!" moment looked different. Maybe it was a phone call, a diagnosis, a conversation that split your life into before and after. Maybe it was something that happened to you, not chosen by you. Maybe it was news that should have been exciting but felt terrifying. Or maybe, like me, it hit you in the smallest moment, standing somewhere ordinary, realizing nothing would ever be ordinary again.

Whatever brought you here, I want you to know something: God is close to you right now. Not watching from a distance. Close. Present. Near to your broken heart.

You do not have to pretend it does not hurt. You do not have to rush past this moment. You just have to let yourself be here, in the "What?!", and know that you are not alone.

Sit With This:

What is your "What?!" moment? What happened that brought you to this devotional? Write it down, even if it is messy. Even if you do not have all the words yet.

____

____

____

____

____

____

____

____

Carry This Forward:

Lord, You are close to the brokenhearted. That means You are close to me right now. Help me believe it. Help me feel it. I do not have to have this figured out today. I just have to let You be near.

In Jesus' name,
AMEN.

Day 2

> "I remember my affliction and my wandering, the bitterness and the gall. I well remember them, and my soul is downcast within me."
>
> **Lamentations 3:19-20 (NIV)**

There is a kind of remembering that happens after everything changes. It is not the nostalgic kind, where you smile at old photographs. It is the intrusive kind, where memories flash without permission and your body responds before your mind catches up.

The writer of Lamentations knew this kind of remembering. He did not pretend the affliction away. He named it. Bitterness. Gall. A downcast soul.

We often rush past this part. We want to skip to the "good part", the hopeful verses, the ones about God's mercies being new every morning. And those verses are true. But they come after this one. The hope comes after the honest naming of pain.

Today, we are not skipping ahead. We are letting ourselves remember. Not to wallow, but to acknowledge. What happened to you was real. The impact is real. And God can hold all of it.

Sit With This:

What do you keep remembering? What moments replay in your mind? Write them here. Not to relive the trauma, but to name it so it does not have to live unnamed inside you.

____

____

____

____

____

____

____

____

____

____

____

Carry This Forward:

Father, You see what I keep remembering. You know the moments that replay in my mind. I am not hiding them from You. Help me release them into Your hands, one memory at a time.
In Jesus' name,
AMEN.

Day 3

> "There is a time for everything, and a season for every activity under the heavens... a time to weep and a time to laugh, a time to mourn and a time to dance."
>
> **Ecclesiastes 3:1, 4 (NIV)**

We live in a culture that wants us to skip the weeping and get straight to the dancing. People mean well when they say things like "everything happens for a reason" or "God has a plan." But sometimes those words land too soon, before we have had permission to simply be sad.

Here is the truth: there is a time to weep. It is not weakness. It is not lack of faith. It is wisdom. It is recognizing that something significant has happened and it deserves to be mourned.

The same God who promises joy in the morning also created tear ducts. He bottles our tears (Psalm 56:8). He does not rush us through our grief.

If you need to weep today, weep. This is not a failure. This is honoring the weight of what you are carrying.

Sit With This:

Have you given yourself permission to grieve? Or have you been rushing toward "feeling better"? What would it look like to let yourself be in this season without apologizing for it?

____

____

____

____

____

____

____

____

____

____

____

____

Carry This Forward:

God, I release myself from the pressure to be okay. If this is my season to weep, I will weep. Thank You for not rushing me. Thank You for holding space for my grief.
In Jesus' name,
AMEN.

Day 4

> "How long, Lord? Will you forget me forever? How long will you hide your face from me? How long must I wrestle with my thoughts and day after day have sorrow in my heart?"
>
> **Psalm 13:1-2 (NIV)**

David was not afraid to ask hard questions. He did not sanitize his prayers. He brought his raw, desperate "how long?" straight to God.

Maybe you are asking that same question. How long will this hurt? How long until I feel normal again? How long until I can breathe without this weight on my chest?

The beautiful thing about David's psalm is that God did not strike him down for asking. The question was not disrespectful, it was relationship. David trusted God enough to bring his frustration, his impatience, his sorrow.

Trust God today and know you can bring yours to Him, too.

Sit With This:

What is your "how long" question today? What are you waiting for? What feels like it is taking forever? Be honest with God. He can handle it.

____

____

____

____

____

____

____

____

____

____

____

Carry This Forward:

Lord, how long? You know what I am waiting for. You know what feels endless right now. I bring my impatience to You, not to demand an answer, but because I trust You with my honest heart. Thank you for being my safe place for all of my emotions and for being a caring father.
In Jesus' name,
AMEN.

Day 5

> "What I feared has come upon me; what I dreaded has happened to me. I have no peace, no quietness; I have no rest, but only turmoil."
>
> **Job 3:25-26 (NIV)**

Sometimes the "What?!" moment is something we secretly feared. We hoped it would never happen, maybe even prayed against it, and then it happened anyway.

Job knew this. His worst-case scenario became his reality. And he did not pretend to be at peace when he was not. He named the turmoil. He acknowledged the restlessness.

If your worst fear has come true, you are not alone. If the thing you prayed would never happen has happened, you are not alone. And you do not have to pretend you have peace when everything inside you is chaos.

God meets us in the turmoil, not just in the calm.

Sit With This:

Was your "What?!" moment something you feared? Did you see it coming, or did it blindside you? How does it feel to be living in the reality you hoped would never arrive?

____

____

____

____

____

____

____

____

____

____

Carry This Forward:

Father, the thing I feared has happened. I do not have peace right now. I do not have quiet. I bring my turmoil to You, trusting that You are not afraid of my chaos. Meet me here. Your Word says you will never leave nor forsake me, Lord. Meet me now.
In Jesus' name,
AMEN.

Day 6

> "God heard the boy crying, and the angel of God called to Hagar from heaven and said to her, 'What is the matter, Hagar? Do not be afraid; God has heard the boy crying as he lies there."
>
> **Job 3:25-26 (NIV)**

Hagar was alone in the wilderness with her son. She had been cast out. She had no resources, no plan, no rescue in sight. She put her child under a bush because she could not bear to watch him die.

And God heard.

Not just her prayers but the text says He heard the boy crying. He heard the raw sound of human distress. He responded not with theology but with presence: "What is the matter, Hagar?"

God is asking you the same question today. Not because He does not know. But because naming what is the matter is part of how we let Him in.

Sit With This:

If God asked you right now, "What is the matter?" How would you answer? Not the Sunday school answer. The real one. What is the matter?

____

____

____

____

____

____

____

____

____

____

____

____

Carry This Forward:

God, You hear me. Not just my prayers, but my crying. You see what is the matter. I am going to tell You anyway, because naming it is how I let You in. Here is what is the matter... Thank you for caring for me and responding to my distress.

In Jesus' name,
AMEN.

Day 7

> "Be still, and know that I am God."
>
> **Psalm 46:10 (NKJV)**

We have spent a week naming what happened. Today, we rest.

Not because the work is done. Not because everything is resolved. But because stillness is part of the process. We cannot keep digging forever. Sometimes we have to pause, breathe, and remember that God is still God... even in this.

"Be still" does not mean "feel peaceful." Your heart might still be racing. Your mind might still be spinning. Stillness is a choice to stop striving, even for a moment. To stop trying to fix, solve, or figure out.

Just for today, let yourself be still. Let God be God.

Sit With This:

What would it look like to be still today? Not to solve anything. Not to plan anything. Just to be. Write down one way you can practice stillness in the next 24 hours.

____

____

____

____

Week One Reflection:

Look back at what you wrote this week. What did you name?
What surprised you? What feels a little lighter for having been
spoken?

____

____

____

____

____

____

____

____

____

____

____

____

Carry This Forward:

*Lord, I am choosing to be still. Not because I have peace, but
because I choose to stop striving. You are God, even in this.
That is enough for today. I know that with You, all things will
work out in due time because You are working it out.*
In Jesus' name,
AMEN.

Week Two

What Am I Feeling?

Day 8

> "Why, my soul, are you downcast? Why so disturbed within me?"
>
> **Psalm 42:5 (NIV)**

The psalmist asks himself a question we often avoid: Why do I feel this way? This week, we are going to do the work of emotional identification. Not to judge our feelings but to understand them. Because what we can name, we can bring to God. What we can identify, we can process.

n therapy, we distinguish between primary and secondary emotions. A primary emotion is the first, most immediate response, it's often something vulnerable like hurt, fear, or sadness. A secondary emotion is what we layer on top, often something that feels safer to express, like anger or numbness.

For example, someone cuts you off in traffic. The secondary emotion might be anger. But underneath, the primary emotion might be fear, you felt unsafe for a moment.

Understanding this distinction helps us get to the root of what we are actually experiencing.

Sit With This:

What emotion have you been most aware of since your "What?!" moment? Write it down. Then ask yourself: Is this the surface emotion or the deeper one? What might be underneath it?

____

____

____

____

____

____

____

____

____

____

____

Carry This Forward:

God, You created me with emotions, all of them. Help me understand what I am feeling, not to judge myself, but to bring my whole heart to You.
In Jesus' name,
AMEN.

Day 9

> "My soul is overwhelmed with sorrow to the point of death."
> **Mark 14:34 (NIV)**

Jesus said these words in the Garden of Gethsemane, hours before His crucifixion. He did not minimize His emotional state. He did not say He was "fine" or "trusting God" (though He was). He named the depth of His sorrow.

Overwhelmed. To the point of death.

If Jesus could name His emotions with that kind of honesty, so can we.

Today, I want you to move beyond general labels. Not just "sad" or "stressed." What specific shade of emotion are you experiencing? Overwhelmed? Exhausted? Betrayed? Abandoned? Relieved but guilty about the relief? Numb? Hypervigilant?

Precision matters. The more specifically we can name what we feel, the more effectively we can process it.

Sit With This:

Circle any emotions you recognize in yourself right now:

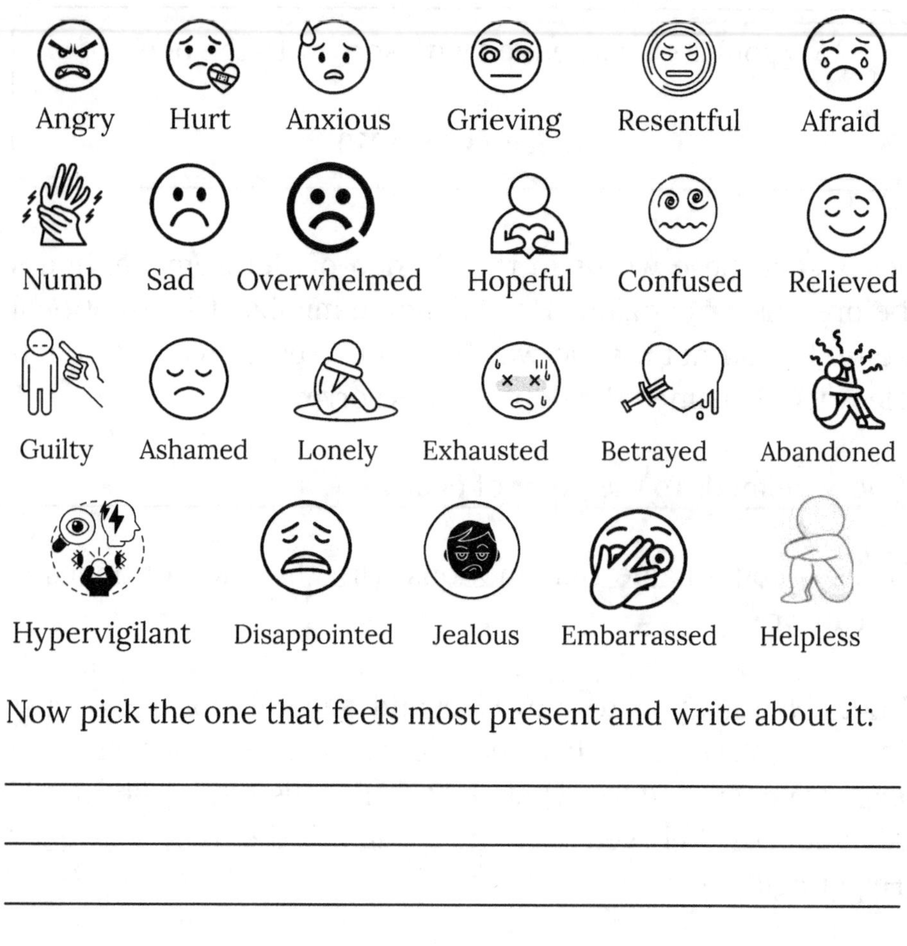

Now pick the one that feels most present and write about it:

____

____

____

____

Carry This Forward:

Jesus, You named Your sorrow honestly. Help me name mine. I do not have to perform strength for You. I can bring my real emotions, specifically and without shame. Thank you for modeling that for me and guiding me through recognizing my own.

**In Jesus' name,
AMEN.**

Day 10

> "Each heart knows its own bitterness, and no one else can share its joy."
> **Proverbs 14:10 (NIV)**

There is a loneliness to experiencing intense emotion. Even when people love us, even when they try to understand, there is a part of our experience that only we know fully.

This is not a failing of your community. It is simply the nature of being human. Each heart knows its own bitterness. And its own joy.

Today, I want you to acknowledge the parts of your experience that feel unshareable. Not because you should carry them alone forever, but because naming the loneliness is part of processing it.

God sees those parts too. The emotions you have not told anyone. The fears you have not admitted. The thoughts you are ashamed of. He knows your heart completely—and He does not turn away.

Sit With This:

What parts of your emotional experience have you not shared with anyone? What feels too complicated, too dark, or too confusing to explain? You do not have to share it with another person yet—but write it here, between you and God.

———————————————————————————

———————————————————————————

———————————————————————————

———————————————————————————

———————————————————————————

———————————————————————————

———————————————————————————

———————————————————————————

———————————————————————————

———————————————————————————

———————————————————————————

Carry This Forward:

Lord, You know my entire heart: the parts I share and the parts I hide. Nothing shocks You. Nothing makes You turn away. I bring the unshareable parts to You today.
In Jesus' name,
AMEN.

Day 11

"I do not understand what I do. For what I want to do I do not do, but what I hate I do."
Romans 7:15 (NIV)

Paul captures something true about the human experience: we are often mysteries to ourselves. And in seasons of disruption, this can intensify. We might react in ways that surprise us: snapping at people we love. Withdrawing when we need connection. Saying yes when we mean no. Finding ourselves unable to do simple things that used to be automatic.

This is not weakness. It is the nervous system responding to overwhelming circumstances. When we are under stress, our usual coping mechanisms can break down.

Today, practice curiosity instead of judgment. When you notice yourself doing something that does not make sense, ask why instead of berating yourself. There is usually a reason, even if it is buried.

Sit With This:

What have you been doing lately that does not make sense to you? What behaviors have surprised you, either things you cannot seem to do or things you cannot seem to stop? Approach this with curiosity, not criticism.

____

____

____

____

____

____

____

____

____

____

____

____

Carry This Forward:

Father, I do not always understand myself. Help me be curious instead of critical. Help me extend grace to myself as I navigate this season. You understand me even when I do not.
In Jesus' name,
AMEN.

Day 12

Notice how physical this description is. Eyes growing weak. Body consumed. Bones weakening.

Emotions are not just mental experiences, they live in our bodies. Grief can settle in our shoulders. Anxiety can grip our stomachs. Sadness can make us physically tired in a way that sleep does not fix.

Today, pay attention to where your emotions are showing up physically. This is not imaginary or dramatic. It is how God made us! We are integrated beings where spirit, soul and body are connected.

Sit With This:

Where do you feel your emotions in your body right now? Scan from your head to your feet. Is there tension? Heaviness? Tightness? Numbness? Write down what you notice.

____

____

____

____

____

____

____

____

____

Now place your hand on that part of your body and take three slow breaths. You do not have to fix anything, just acknowledge it.

Carry This Forward:

Lord, You see how this season is affecting my body. You care about my physical well-being, not just my spiritual state. Help me care for my body as part of caring for my soul.
In Jesus' name,
AMEN.

Day 13

"The heart is deceitful above all things and beyond cure. Who can understand it? I the Lord search the heart and examine the mind."

Jeremiah 17:9-10 (NIV)

Sometimes the first emotion we feel is not the truest one. Anger often sits on top of hurt. Anxiety often covers grief. Resentment can mask fear.

On day 8 we talked about these secondary emotions. It's important to know that secondary emotions are real, but they are not the root. They are the branches waving in the wind like flags to get our attention while something deeper anchors—or uproots—the whole tree.

Today, I want you to look beneath. Not to dismiss what you are feeling on the surface, but to ask what is underneath it. God is not afraid of your layers. He is not fooled by them either. He searches the heart. He examines the mind. Not to condemn, but to heal.

What if you let Him look with you?

Sit With This:

What emotion have you been feeling most strongly this week?

____

____

____

Now ask yourself: What is underneath that? Now, if you peeled that back, what would you find?

____

____

____

Roots Check:

Circle any emotions you recognize in yourself today:

 Angry

 Hurt

 Anxious

 Grieving

 Resentful

 Afraid

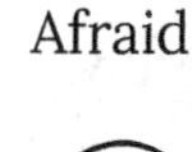  

Numb Sad Overwhelmed Hopeful Confused Relieved

 Guilty

 Ashamed

 Lonely

Carry This Forward:

Lord, search my heart. Show me what is underneath. I trust You with what You find.
In Jesus' name,
AMEN.

Day 14

> "We do not want you to be uninformed, brothers and sisters, about the troubles we experienced in the province of Asia. We were under great pressure, far beyond our ability to endure, so that we despaired of life itself. Indeed, we felt we had received the sentence of death."
>
> **2 Corinthians 1:8-9 (NIV)**

Paul does not sugarcoat his experience. He admits to despair. To pressure beyond what he could endure. To feeling like death was certain.

And he wrote these words in Scripture. Inspired by the Holy Spirit. Which means God wanted us to know that even the apostle Paul had seasons where he despaired of life itself.

Today, we rest in this truth: despair is not disqualification. Feeling overwhelmed does not mean you lack faith. The same Paul who wrote about hope and perseverance also wrote about reaching his breaking point.

If you are at your breaking point, you are in good company.

Sit With This:

Have you reached a breaking point in this season? What does despair look like for you, not as a theological concept, but as a lived experience? It is okay to name it.

____

____

____

____

Week Two Reflection:

What have you learned about your emotional landscape this week? Which emotions surprised you? Which ones feel more understandable now that you have named them?

____

____

____

____

Carry This Forward:

God, thank You for including despair in Scripture. Thank You for not hiding the breaking points of Your people. I bring my despair to You, trusting that it does not disqualify me from Your love or Your plans.
In Jesus' name,
AMEN.

Week Three

What Am I Afraid Of?

Day 15

> "So do not fear, for I am with you; do not be dismayed, for I am your God. I will strengthen you and help you; I will uphold you with my righteous right hand."
>
> **Isaiah 41:10 (NIV)**

Fear is often the undercurrent beneath all our other emotions. When everything changes, fear rushes in to fill the uncertainty.

This week, we are going to name our fears. Not to give them more power, but to bring them into the light where God can meet them.

Notice that Isaiah does not say "do not fear because nothing bad will happen." He says "do not fear because I am with you." The comfort is not the absence of difficulty. The comfort comes from the presence of God in the midst of the difficulty.

Your fears may be completely rational given what you have experienced. But they do not have the final word. God does!

Sit With This:

What are you most afraid of right now? Make a list, as long as it needs to be. Some fears will be big and existential. Some will be small and specific. Write them all.

____

____

____

____

____

____

____

____

____

____

____

____

____

Carry This Forward:

Lord, I am afraid. Here is my list. I bring these fears to You, not because they will magically disappear, but because You promised to be with me. Help me to feel and magnify Your presence even in the midst of my fear.
In Jesus' name,
AMEN.

Day 16

> "When I am afraid, I put my trust in you. In God, whose word I praise—in God I trust and am not afraid. What can mere mortals do to me?"
>
> **Psalm 56:3-4 (NIV)**

David says "when I am afraid," not "if I am afraid." Fear is assumed. It is part of the human experience, especially when we face opposition or uncertainty.

What David does with fear is instructive. He does not deny it. He does not rebuke it. He redirects it. "When I am afraid, I put my trust in you."

Trust does not mean we stop feeling fear. It means we choose where to place our weight while we are afraid. We lean into God instead of spiraling into worst-case scenarios.

Today, practice this redirection. Every time fear rises, acknowledge it, then consciously shift your weight toward trust.

Sit With This:

Look at the fears you listed yesterday. Choose one specific fear. Write it below:

____

____

____

____

Now, write a trust statement next to it. "When I am afraid of
_______________, I put my trust in God who
_______________."

____

____

____

____

____

____

Carry This Forward:

God, I am afraid. And I am choosing to put my trust in You. Not because the fear is gone, but because You are bigger. Help me keep redirecting.
In Jesus' name,
AMEN.

Day 17

> "Therefore do not worry about tomorrow, for tomorrow will worry about itself. Each day has enough trouble of its own."
>
> **Matthew 6:34 (NIV)**

I walked across the stage at my Graduate College graduation with a Master's degree in my hand and a question in my heart: Now what?

I had been a student for as long as I could remember. That identity shaped my days, my schedule, my sense of purpose. And suddenly it was over. I sat at home the next morning and thought, "So I am not a student anymore. Who am I?"

The fear was not about a specific threat. It was about the vast, undefined future stretching out in front of me. I did not know what came next. I did not have a clear plan. And that uncertainty felt like a kind of freefall.

Maybe your "What?!" moment includes this fear of the unknown. Not just what happened, but what happens now. The future that once felt planned or predictable is now a question mark.

Jesus reminds us: each day has enough trouble of its own. We do not have to solve tomorrow, today. We just have to show up for today.

Sit With This:

What uncertainties about the future are weighing on you? What "Now what?" questions keep you up at night?

____

____

____

____

____

Now practice Jesus' instruction: For today, release those questions. What is the one thing you need to focus on today? Yup.. just today.

____

____

____

____

____

Carry This Forward:

Father, I am scared of what I cannot see. Help me release tomorrow and show up for today. Give me grace for the next 24 hours. That is all I need right now.
In Jesus' name,
AMEN.

Day 18

"For the Spirit God gave us does not make us timid, but gives us power, love and self-discipline."

2 Timothy 1:7 (NIV)

Fear can make us shrink. It can make us pull back, play small, avoid anything that feels risky. In psychology, we call this avoidance behavior and it makes sense. If something feels dangerous, our instinct is to stay away.

But avoidance can become a prison. When we arrange our entire lives around what we are afraid of, fear wins.

Paul reminds Timothy that the Spirit we have been given is not a spirit of timidity. It is a spirit of power, love, and self-discipline. This does not mean we will not feel fear. It means fear does not get to dictate our choices.

Today, notice where fear might be shrinking your life. What are you avoiding? What feels too scary to attempt?

Sit With This:

What have you been avoiding because of fear? What conversations, decisions, or actions feel too risky to attempt?

____

____

____

____

____

Choose one small thing you have been avoiding. What would it look like to take one tiny step toward it, not the whole thing, just one step?

____

____

____

____

____

Carry This Forward:

Lord, I do not want fear to shrink my life. Give me power where I feel weak. Give me love where I feel defensive. Give me self-discipline where I feel chaotic. Help me take one step today.
In Jesus' name,
AMEN.

Day 19

> "There is no fear in love. But perfect love drives out fear, because fear has to do with punishment. The one who fears is not made perfect in love."
>
> **1 John 4:18 (NIV)**

Fear and love cannot fully coexist. Where love expands, fear contracts. Where fear dominates, love struggles to flourish.

I learned this during the season when I was struggling to put my son to bed most nights. He would cry himself to sleep, and I would cry right along with him on the other side of the door. I was terrified. Terrified that I would not be able to do this parenting thing successfully. Terrified that I could not be both the entrepreneur and the successful single parent, bringing in enough income to pay for all the bills and childcare by myself.

That season was my turning point.

Part of fear's power is its insistence that we are alone. That if things go wrong, we will be abandoned. That we have to figure this out by ourselves.

Love contradicts all of that. God's love says: You are not alone. You will not be abandoned. You do not have to figure this out by yourself.

Sit With This:

Which fears are connected to a belief that you are alone or will be abandoned? How might God's love speak to those specific fears?

____

____

____

____

____

____

____

____

____

____

____

Carry This Forward:

Father, drive out my fear with Your love. Help me feel Your presence so deeply that fear loses its grip. I am not alone. I am loved.
In Jesus' name,
AMEN.

Day 20

> "Even though I walk through the darkest valley, I will fear no evil, for you are with me; your rod and your staff, they comfort me."
>
> **Psalm 23:4 (NKJV)**

Notice the preposition: through. David does not say he walks around the valley or avoids it entirely. He walks through it.

The valley is real. The darkness is real. But it is not a destination—it is a passage. We are walking through, not camping out.

And in the walking, we are not alone. The Shepherd's rod and staff are protective and guiding. Even in the darkest valley, there is presence. There is comfort.

Today, hold onto that word: through. This valley is not forever. You are passing through.

Sit With This:

What does your darkest valley look like right now? Describe it,not to wallow, but to acknowledge where you are walking.

____

____

____

____

____

____

Now remind yourself: This is a passage, not a destination. What would it feel like to trust that you are walking through, not stuck in?

____

____

____

____

____

____

Carry This Forward:

Lord, I am in the valley. But I am walking through, not stuck. Your rod and staff are with me. Help me feel Your presence as my comfort and my guide.
In Jesus' name,
AMEN.

Day 21

"The Lord himself goes before you and will be with you; he will never leave you nor forsake you. Do not be afraid; do not be discouraged."

Deuteronomy 31:8 (NIV)

Moses speaks these words to Joshua, who is about to lead the Israelites into unknown territory. Joshua has every reason to be afraid. The task ahead is massive. The obstacles are real. And Moses, his mentor, is dying.

The comfort Moses offers is not "this will be easy" or "nothing will go wrong." It is "God goes before you."

Whatever you are walking into,whatever unknown territory your "What?!" moment has created, God is already there. He goes before you. He is with you. He will not leave you.

Today, we rest in this promise as we close our week of naming fears.

Sit With This:

What unknown territory are you walking into? What is ahead that feels scary?

____

____

____

____

Whatever brought you here, I want you to know something: God is close to you right now. Not watching from a distance. Close. Present. Near to your broken heart.

You do not have to pretend it does not hurt. You do not have to rush past this moment. You just have to let yourself be here, in the "What?!", and know that you are not alone.

Sit With This:

What is your "What?!" moment? What happened that brought you to this devotional? Write it down, even if it is messy. Even if you do not have all the words yet.

____

____

____

____

____

____

____

Carry This Forward:

Lord, You are close to the brokenhearted. That means You are close to me right now. Help me believe it. Help me feel it. I do not have to have this figured out today. I just have to let You be near.

**In Jesus' name,
AMEN.**

Now imagine God already there, preparing the way. What would it change if you really believed He goes before you?

____

____

____

____

Week Three Reflection:

Look back at the fears you have named this week. Which ones feel smaller after bringing them to God? Which ones still feel heavy? There is no wrong answer—just notice.

____

____

____

____

____

____

____

Carry This Forward:

Lord, You go before me. You are with me. You will never leave me. I choose to believe this even when I cannot feel it. Do not let me be afraid or discouraged.

In Jesus' name,
AMEN.

Week Four

Where Is God In This?

Day 22

> "You have searched me, Lord, and you know me. You know when I sit and when I rise; you perceive my thoughts from afar. You discern my going out and my lying down; you are familiar with all my ways. Before a word is on my tongue you, Lord, know it completely."
>
> **Psalm 139:1-4 (NIV)**

In the chaos of change, it is easy to feel invisible. Like no one really sees what you are going through. Like you are carrying something too heavy to be fully witnessed.

But God sees. Completely.

I felt this during the time when my son was being assessed for and diagnosed with level 3 Autism. Aside from the hours-long assessment appointments and parent-led therapy sessions multiple times a week, the day-to-day presentation of symptoms turned our lives on its head. I was drowning in logistics, advocacy, grief, and hope all tangled together. Most people in my life only saw pieces of it. No one could see the whole picture.

But God was not oblivious to what was going on.

He knows when you sit down, exhausted. When you get up, summoning energy you do not have. He perceives your thoughts, even the ones you cannot articulate. He is familiar with all your ways.

This week, we are anchoring ourselves in who God is. Not abstract theology, but the specific aspects of His character that meet us in seasons like this. Today, we start with His omniscience, His complete knowledge.

You are fully known. Nothing about your situation is hidden from Him. Nothing surprises Him. And knowing all of it, He still draws near.

Sit With This:

What does it feel like to be fully known? Does it comfort you or unsettle you (or both)? What parts of your current experience do you most need God to see?

____

____

____

____

____

____

____

____

Carry This Forward:

Lord, You know me completely! You know every thought, every fear, every hope, every hidden thing. Thank You for not turning away. Help me rest in being fully known and fully loved.

In Jesus' name,
AMEN.

Day 23

> "God is our refuge and strength, an ever-present help in trouble. Therefore we will not fear, though the earth give way and the mountains fall into the heart of the sea."
>
> **Psalm 46:1-2 (NIV)**

An ever-present help. Not an occasional help. Not a help that shows up sometimes. Ever present.

The imagery here is apocalyptic: the earth giving way, mountains falling into the sea. This is not a minor inconvenience. This is everything collapsing. And even in that, God IS refuge. God IS strength. God IS present.

When your "What?!" moment made everything feel like it was collapsing, God did not step back. He stepped in. He is stepping in now.

Today, meditate on God as refuge. A refuge is a place of safety, a shelter from the storm. Where can you feel His shelter today?

Sit With This:

What does God as refuge mean to you in this specific season?
How do you need Him to shelter you right now?

____

____

____

____

____

____

____

____

____

____

____

Carry This Forward:

_Father, be my refuge today. Be my shelter when everything feels
unstable. You are ever present! Help me experience that
presence as protection._
In Jesus' name,
AMEN.

Day 24

This verse can be weaponized. "Everything happens for a reason" can feel like a dismissal of pain when it is offered too quickly, without sitting in the grief first.

But properly understood, this is not a dismissal, it is a promise about God's character. He is a God who redeems. Who takes broken things and weaves them into something purposeful.

This does not mean your pain was good. It does not mean God caused your suffering. It means He refuses to waste it. He is at work, even now, turning what was meant for harm into something that will serve His purposes.

Today, hold this truth loosely. You do not have to see the "good" yet. You just have to trust the One who promises to work it.

Sit With This:

Has anyone offered you Romans 8:28 in a way that felt dismissive? What did you need to hear instead?

____

____

____

____

____

Now, read the verse again, slowly. What does it offer you when you are ready to receive it?

____

____

____

____

____

____

Carry This Forward:

God, I trust that You are working, even when I cannot see it. I do not need to understand the good yet, I just need to trust the One who promised it. Work in my situation, Lord.
In Jesus' name,
AMEN.

Day 25

God is a healer. This is not just His function, it is His nature. He moves toward broken hearts. He binds wounds.

Healing is not the same as erasing. A bound wound still happened. A healed heart still carries the memory. But binding and healing mean we are not left open and bleeding forever.

Today, let yourself receive this aspect of God's character. He is not standing at a distance, evaluating whether you deserve healing. He is moving toward you, bandages in hand, ready to bind what is broken.

Sit With This:

Where do you most need healing right now? Name the specific wounds: emotional, relational, and spiritual, that you want God to bind.

____

____

____

____

____

____

____

____

____

____

____

Carry This Forward:

Healer, I am wounded. You know where the breaks are. Bind me up, Lord. Not erasing what happened, but healing what is broken.
In Jesus' name,
AMEN.

Day 26

> "Because of the Lord's great love we are not consumed,
> though his compassions never fail. They are new every
> morning; great is your faithfulness."
>
> **Lamentations 3:22-23 (NIV)**

Lamentations is a book of grief. The writer has witnessed the destruction of Jerusalem, the exile of his people, and unimaginable loss. And in the middle of that grief, he writes these words.

Not consumed. Even in devastation, he notices that he is still here. Still breathing. Still being given new compassion every morning.

This is not toxic positivity. This is radical noticing in the midst of suffering. Acknowledging that even in the worst seasons, there is mercy keeping us from being completely destroyed.

Today, practice this radical noticing. What has kept you from being consumed? Where is the mercy showing up?

Sit With This:

What has kept you from being consumed in this season? What mercies, even small ones, have shown up?

____

____

____

____

____

____

____

____

____

____

____

Carry This Forward:

Lord, I am not consumed. Even in this, Your compassions have not failed. Help me notice the new mercies today. Great is Your faithfulness.
In Jesus' name,
AMEN.

Day 27

> "For we do not have a high priest who is unable to empathize with our weaknesses, but we have one who has been tempted in every way, just as we are—yet he did not sin. Let us then approach God's throne of grace with confidence, so that we may receive mercy and find grace to help us in our time of need."
>
> **Hebrews 4:15-16 (NIV)**

Jesus knows what it is to suffer. He was not protected from pain. He did not float above human experience. He was tempted. He grieved. He felt abandoned.

This means when we approach Him, we are not approaching someone who cannot understand. We have a high priest who empathizes, who has felt what we feel.

Today, approach the throne of grace with confidence. Not confidence in yourself, but confidence in His mercy. He is not rolling His eyes at your weakness. He is meeting it with grace.

Sit With This:

How does it change things to know that Jesus empathizes with your weaknesses? That He has felt temptation, grief, and pain?

____

____

____

____

____

What do you need to bring to the throne of grace today with confidence?

____

____

____

____

____

____

____

Carry This Forward:

What do you need to bring to the throne of grace today with confidence?
In Jesus' name,
AMEN.

Day 28

"Do not fear, for I have redeemed you; I have summoned you by name; you are mine. When you pass through the waters, I will be with you; and when you pass through the rivers, they will not sweep over you. When you walk through the fire, you will not be burned; the flames will not set you ablaze."

Isaiah 43:1-2 (NIV)

Three times in these verses: through.

Through the waters. Through the rivers. Through the fire.

Not around. Not over. Through.

God does not promise to eliminate the hard passages. He promises to be with us in them. The waters may rise. The rivers may rush. The fire may rage. But we are not alone. We are His. He has called us by name.

Whatever you are passing through, you belong to Him.

Sit With This:

What waters, rivers, or fires are you passing through right now? Name them specifically.

____

____

____

____

____

Now hear God speak your name and say: "You are Mine. I am with you in this." How does that land?

____

____

____

____

____

____

____

____

Carry This Forward:

God, I am passing through waters. Through fire. But You have called me by name. I am Yours. Be with me today. Do not let me be swept away or burned.
In Jesus' name,
AMEN.

Day 29-30

For the final two days of Part One, we are going to do something different. These days are designed for deeper engagement with Scripture. Not reading a devotional thought from me, but letting God's Word speak directly to you.

Below, you will find twenty scriptures. These verses speak to being seen, being known, and being held in uncertain seasons. Your task over these two days is to read through all twenty, then highlight two or three that speak most directly to where you are right now.

Do not rush this. Read slowly. Let the words wash over you. Notice which ones make you pause. Which ones make you want to cry. Which ones make you breathe a little deeper.

Those are your verses. Mark them. Memorize them. Return to them.

List of Scriptures on Being Seen

"She gave this name to the Lord who spoke to her: "You are the God who sees me," for she said, "I have now seen the One who sees me."

Genesis 16:13 (NIV)

"The Lord is close to the brokenhearted and saves those who are crushed in spirit."

Psalm 34:18(NIV)

"You keep track of all my sorrows. You have collected all my tears in your bottle. You have recorded each one in your book."

Psalm 56:8(NLT)

"Where can I go from your Spirit? Where can I flee from your presence? If I go up to the heavens, you are there; if I make my bed in the depths, you are there. If I rise on the wings of the dawn, if I settle on the far side of the sea, even there your hand will guide me, your right hand will hold me fast."

Psalm 139:7-10 (NIV)

"The Lord is near to all who call on him, to all who call on him in truth."

Psalm 145:18 (NIV)

"So do not fear, for I am with you; do not be dismayed, for I am your God. I will strengthen you and help you; I will uphold you with my righteous right hand."

Isaiah 41:10(NIV)

"The Lord is close to the brokenhearted and saves those who are crushed in spirit."
Psalm 34:18(NIV)

"And even the very hairs of your head are all numbered. So don't be afraid; you are worth more than many sparrows."
Matthew 10:30-31(NLT)

"Come to me, all you who are weary and burdened, and I will give you rest. Take my yoke upon you and learn from me, for I am gentle and humble in heart, and you will find rest for your souls. For my yoke is easy and my burden is light."
Matthew 11:28-30 (NIV)

"The gatekeeper opens the gate for him, and the sheep listen to his voice. He calls his own sheep by name and leads them out. When he has brought out all his own, he goes on ahead of them, and his sheep follow him because they know his voice."
John 10:3-4(NIV)

"I will not leave you as orphans; I will come to you."
John 14:18 (NIV)

"For I am convinced that neither death nor life, neither angels nor demons, neither the present nor the future, nor any powers, neither height nor depth, nor anything else in all creation, will be able to separate us from the love of God that is in Christ Jesus our Lord."

Romans 8:38-39 (NIV)

"We are hard pressed on every side, but not crushed; perplexed, but not in despair; persecuted, but not abandoned; struck down, but not destroyed."

2 Corinthians 4:8-9 (NIV)

"Do not be anxious about anything, but in every situation, by prayer and petition, with thanksgiving, present your requests to God. And the peace of God, which transcends all understanding, will guard your hearts and your minds in Christ Jesus."

Philippians 4:6-7 (NIV)

"Cast all your anxiety on him because he cares for you."

1 Peter 5:7 (NIV)

"He will wipe every tear from their eyes. There will be no more death or mourning or crying or pain, for the old order of things has passed away."

Revelation 21:4 (NIV)

Day 29

Read and Receive

Today, read through all twenty scriptures slowly. Do not analyze. Just receive. Notice which ones make you pause.

Which three scriptures spoke most directly to you today?

1. ____

____

2. ____

____

3. ____

____

Why these three? What did they stir in you?

____

____

____

____

____

____

Carry This Forward:

Lord, Your Word is alive. Let it take root in me. Let these verses become anchors for my soul.
In Jesus' name,
AMEN.

Day 30

Return and Reflect

Today, return to the three scriptures you highlighted yesterday. Read them again. Write them out by hand below—there is something powerful about physically writing Scripture.

Scripture 1:

Scripture 2:

Scripture 3:

Part One: Reflection

You have completed the first thirty days. You have acknowledged what happened, named your emotions, faced your fears, and anchored yourself in who God is.

Look back at the journey. What surprised you? What shifted? What still feels heavy?

____

____

____

____

____

____

____

____

What is one truth you want to carry into Part Two?

____

____

____

____

____

____

____

Part Two: Attend

> "Search me, O God, and know my heart."
> **Psalm 139:23 (NIV)**

You have done the brave work of acknowledgment. You have named what happened, identified your emotions, faced your fears, and anchored yourself in who God is.

Now we go deeper.

Part Two is about attending: paying close attention to what is being revealed. When life shakes us, it often exposes things that were hidden: beliefs we did not know we held, wounds we thought were healed, foundations that were weaker than we realized.

This is not punishment. This is an invitation. God uses disruption to show us what needs tending at our roots. The circumstances are the fruit we can see, but the roots determine what kind of fruit will grow next.

Over the next thirty days, we will examine what we believed before, what is being uprooted, who is with us, and what God says about our identity. This is sacred excavation. It requires courage and gentleness in equal measure.

You have already proven you can do hard things. Let us continue.

Week Five

What Did I Believe Before?

Day 31

Everything flows from the heart. Our actions, our reactions, our hopes, our fears—all of it springs from what we believe at the deepest level.

Before your "What?!" moment, you held certain beliefs. Some were conscious: "I believe God is good." "I believe hard work pays off." "I believe my marriage will last." Others were unconscious, operating in the background like software you forgot was running.

When life disrupts us, these beliefs get exposed. Some hold firm. Others crack. And some... the ones we did not even know we had, suddenly become visible.

This week, we are going to excavate. What did you believe before everything changed? Not what you said you believed, but what you actually believed, the convictions that shaped how you lived.

Sit With This:

Before your "What?!" moment, what did you believe about your life? About your future? About how things were supposed to go? Write down the beliefs you held, spoken or unspoken.

____

____

____

____

____

____

____

____

____

____

____

____

Carry This Forward:

Lord, show me what I believed before. Not to judge myself, but to understand myself. Help me see the roots that were already there.

In Jesus' name,
AMEN.

Day 32

"But blessed is the one who trusts in the Lord, whose confidence is in him. They will be like a tree planted by the water that sends out its roots by the stream. It does not fear when heat comes; its leaves are always green. It has no worries in a year of drought and never fails to bear fruit."

Jeremiah 17:7-8 (NIV)

A tree planted by water does not fear the heat because its roots reach the stream. The surface conditions matter less when the source is secure.

What was your source before everything changed? Where did your roots reach? Some of us had roots in relationships—our identity came from being someone's spouse, parent, or child. Some had roots in career—our worth was tied to our title or salary. Some had roots in control— we believed we could manage our way to safety.

These are not bad things to value. But when they become our primary source, we are vulnerable to drought.

Today, honestly assess where your roots were planted before your "What?!" moment.

Sit With This:

Before your "What?!" moment, where did your sense of
security come from? Where did your identity come from?
What was the "stream" your roots reached toward?

Carry This Forward:

*God, I want my roots in You. Show me where I was drawing life
from other sources. Not to shame me, but to redirect me toward
the stream that never runs dry.*

**In Jesus' name,
AMEN.**

Day 33

> "Therefore everyone who hears these words of mine and puts them into practice is like a wise man who built his house on the rock. The rain came down, the streams rose, and the winds blew and beat against that house; yet it did not fall, because it had its foundation on the rock."
>
> **Matthew 7:24-25 (NIV)**

Notice: the storm came to both houses in Jesus' parable. The one built on rock and the one built on sand both experienced rain, rising streams, and battering winds. The difference was not the presence of the storm but the foundation beneath.

Your "What?!" moment was a storm. It tested your foundation. Some things held. Some things collapsed. This is not failure, it is information.

What held? What collapsed? The answers reveal what was built on rock and what was built on sand.

Sit With This:

When the storm hit, what held firm? What parts of your faith, your relationships, your sense of self remained standing?

____

____

____

____

____

What collapsed or crumbled? What could not withstand the pressure?

____

____

____

____

____

____

Carry This Forward:

Lord, thank You for what held. Help me rebuild what collapsed on a firmer foundation. Show me what was sand so I can replace it with rock.
In Jesus' name,
AMEN.

Day 34

"For my thoughts are not your thoughts, neither are your ways my ways,' declares the Lord. 'As the heavens are higher than the earth, so are my ways higher than your ways and my thoughts than your thoughts."

Isaiah 55:8-9 (NIV)

Before everything changed, you probably had a picture of how your life would go. Maybe it was detailed: career milestones, family timeline, retirement plans. Maybe it was vague: general happiness, reasonable health, gradual progress.

Either way, you had a script. And your "What?!" moment was not in it.

When our script gets torn up, we face a choice: rage against the Author or trust that He sees what we cannot. This is not easy. It requires holding our plans loosely while gripping His character tightly.

Today, acknowledge the script you had and the grief of watching it change.

Sit With This:

What was your script before? What did you expect your life to look like at this point? Be specific.

____

____

____

____

____

How does it feel to hold that script now? What emotions come up when you compare what you expected to what happened?

____

____

____

____

____

____

Carry This Forward:

Father, my script has been rewritten. I am grieving what I expected. Help me trust that Your thoughts are higher, even when I cannot see the new story You are writing.
In Jesus' name,
AMEN.

Day 35

"Whom have I in heaven but you? And earth has nothing I desire besides you. My flesh and my heart may fail, but God is the strength of my heart and my portion forever."

Psalm 73:25-26 (NIV)

Asaph wrote Psalm 73 after wrestling with doubt. He had watched the wicked prosper while he suffered. He nearly lost his faith. But in the sanctuary of God, his perspective shifted.

He landed here: "Earth has nothing I desire besides you."

This is not a denial of earthly goods. Asaph still needed food, shelter, and relationships. But he recognized that none of those things could be his ultimate portion. Only God could hold that place.

Before your "What?!" moment, what did you desire most? Not what you said you desired, but what you actually oriented your life around?

Sit With This:

What were your deepest desires before everything changed?
What did you want most from life?

____

____

____

____

____

How have those desires shifted since your "What?!" moment?
What do you desire now?

____

____

____

____

____

____

Carry This Forward:

Lord, You are my portion. When everything else fails, You remain. Help me desire You above all else, not as a religious duty, but as the truest longing of my heart.
AMEN.

Day 36

James does not say "consider it pure joy that trials exist." He says consider it joy when you face them because something is being produced.

Trials test faith. Testing produces perseverance. Perseverance produces maturity and completeness.

This does not mean we manufacture happiness about our pain. It means we recognize that something is happening beneath the surface. The "What?!" moment is not just destruction, it is also formation.

What is being formed in you?

Sit With This:

What has your "What?!" moment revealed about your faith? Where was it stronger than you thought? Where was it weaker?

____

____

____

____

____

What might be forming in you through this trial? What perseverance, maturity, or completeness is being developed?

____

____

____

____

____

Carry This Forward:

God, I do not naturally consider trials joy. But I trust that You are producing something in me. Let perseverance finish its work. Make me mature and complete.
AMEN.

Day 36

> "Therefore, since we are surrounded by such a great cloud of witnesses, let us throw off everything that hinders and the sin that so easily entangles. And let us run with perseverance the race marked out for us, fixing our eyes on Jesus, the pioneer and perfecter of faith."
>
> **Hebrews 12:1-2 (NIV)**

Before everything changed, you were carrying things. Some were good such as your gifts, callings, and relationships worth tending. Others were hindrances like the beliefs, habits, patterns that weighed you down but felt too familiar to release.

Disruption has a way of loosening our grip. Things we thought we needed fall away. Sometimes this is loss. Sometimes it is liberation.

As we close this week, take inventory. What were you carrying before that you no longer need to carry?

Sit With This:

What have you been carrying that hinders your race? What beliefs, habits, or patterns were weighing you down before your "What?!" moment?

____

____

____

____

____

____

____

____

What has fallen away since? Was any of it a hidden gift, something you are actually lighter without?

____

____

____

____

____

____

____

Week Five Reflection:

What have you learned about what you believed before? What beliefs were helpful? What beliefs were exposed as insufficient?

____

____

____

____

____

____

____

____

____

____

____

____

____

Carry This Forward:

God, I do not naturally consider trials joy. But I trust that You are producing something in me. Let perseverance finish its work. Make me mature and complete.
In Jesus' name,
AMEN.

Week Six

What Is Being Uprooted?

Day 33

> "See, today I appoint you over nations and kingdoms to uproot and tear down, to destroy and overthrow, to build and to plant."
> **Jeremiah 1:10 (NIV)**

God's work often involves uprooting before planting. Jeremiah was called to both tear down and build up. The destruction was not the end; it was preparation.

Your "What?!" moment has uprooted things. Some of what was torn out needed to go like the beliefs that were not serving you, patterns that were harming you, identities that were too small. Other things were good and their loss is genuine grief.

This week, we look honestly at what is being uprooted. Not to minimize the pain, but to see clearly. What is God removing? What might He be preparing to plant?

Sit With This:

What has been uprooted in your life since your "What?!" moment? List everything: the losses you grieve and the things you might be relieved to release.

____

____

____

____

____

____

____

____

____

____

____

____

____

Carry This Forward:

God, You are doing a work that involves uprooting. Help me trust Your hand even when the tearing is painful. Prepare the soil for what You want to plant.

In Jesus' name,
AMEN.

Day 39

"I am the true vine, and my Father is the gardener. He cuts off every branch in me that bears no fruit, while every branch that does bear fruit he prunes so that it will be even more fruitful."
John 15:1-2 (NIV)

Even fruitful branches get pruned. This is hard to accept. We want to believe that if we do everything right, we will avoid the cutting. But the Gardener knows that pruning is how growth happens.

What if your "What?!" moment is pruning, not punishment? What if something had to be cut so something better could grow?

This does not minimize your pain. Pruning hurts. But it reframes the purpose.

Sit With This:

What if your "What?!" moment is pruning rather than punishment? How does that reframe change how you see what happened?

____

____

____

____

____

What might God be trying to make more fruitful in your life through this cutting?

____

____

____

____

____

____

Carry This Forward:

Father, I trust that You are a good Gardener. Even when the pruning hurts, I believe You are making me more fruitful. Help me submit to Your cutting.
In Jesus' name,
AMEN.

Day 40

> "Therefore we do not lose heart. Though outwardly we are wasting away, yet inwardly we are being renewed day by day. For our light and momentary troubles are producing for us an eternal glory that far outweighs them all. So we fix our eyes not on what is seen, but on what is unseen, since what is seen is temporary, but what is unseen is eternal."
>
> **2 Corinthians 4:16-18 (NIV)**

Paul calls his troubles "light and momentary." This is the same Paul who was shipwrecked, beaten, imprisoned, and left for dead. His troubles were not objectively light. But compared to eternal glory, he could hold them differently.

This is not toxic positivity. It is eternal perspective.

What is visible right now is real and painful. But it is also temporary. What is being produced in the unseen realm will last forever.

Sit With This:

What is wasting away in your life right now? What outward
things are diminishing?

____

____

____

____

____

____

What might be renewing inwardly, even if you cannot fully
see it yet?

____

____

____

____

____

____

Carry This Forward:

*Lord, help me fix my eyes on what is unseen. Renew me
inwardly even as things waste away outwardly. Give me
eternal perspective.*
AMEN.

Day 41

> "Yet you desired faithfulness even in the womb; you taught me wisdom in that secret place."
>
> **Psalm 51:6 (NIV)**

God is interested in the secret places. Your secret places are the parts of us no one else sees. The inner rooms of our hearts where our true beliefs live.

Disruption has a way of exposing those secret places. What we believe about ourselves, about God, about others comes to the surface under pressure.

What has been exposed in you? Not to shame yourself, but to see clearly. What was hiding in the secret place that is now visible?

Sit With This:

What has your "What?!" moment exposed about your inner life? What beliefs, fears, or patterns have come to the surface that were previously hidden?

____

____

____

____

____

How do you feel about what has been exposed? Is there grief? Relief? Shame? Curiosity?

____

____

____

____

____

____

Carry This Forward:

God, You see my secret places. You know what has been exposed. Meet me there. Teach me wisdom in the hidden parts of my heart.
AMEN.

Day 42

David invites God to search him. This is vulnerable. It requires trust that God's searching is for healing, not condemnation.

This week, we have been examining what is being uprooted. Today, we specifically invite God into the process. Instead of just observing what has been exposed, we ask Him to show us what we might still be missing.

This is not self-flagellation. It is partnership with the One who knows us fully and loves us completely.

Sit With This:

Pray Psalm 139:23-24 slowly. Then sit in silence for two minutes. What does God bring to mind?

____

____

____

____

____

Is there anything you sense God uprooting that you have been resisting?

____

____

____

____

____

____

Carry This Forward:

Search me, God. Know my heart. Test me and know my anxious thoughts. Show me what needs to go, and lead me in the way everlasting.
AMEN.

Day 43

> "I will give you a new heart and put a new spirit in you; I will remove from you your heart of stone and give you a heart of flesh."
>
> **Ezekiel 36:26 (NIV)**

God promises to do heart surgery. He removes what has hardened and replaces it with something alive.

Sometimes our hearts harden to protect us. We experienced pain, so we built walls. We were betrayed, so we stopped trusting. We were disappointed, so we lowered our expectations.

These defenses made sense. But they also made us less alive.

What has hardened in you? What stone heart is God wanting to replace?

Sit With This:

Where has your heart hardened? What walls have you built to protect yourself?

____

____

____

____

____

____

What would it look like for God to give you a heart of flesh in those areas—tender, responsive, alive?

____

____

____

____

____

____

Carry This Forward:

Lord, I have built walls. I have let my heart harden. Remove the stone. Give me a heart of flesh. One that is tender, responsive, fully alive to You.
AMEN.

Day 44

> "Forget the former things; do not dwell on the past. See, I am doing a new thing! Now it springs up; do you not perceive it? I am making a way in the wilderness and streams in the wasteland."
> **Isaiah 43:18-19 (NIV)**

God is doing a new thing. But to see it, we sometimes have to stop staring at the old thing.

This does not mean we pretend the past did not happen. It means we do not let it consume all our attention. God is making a way forward—a path in the wilderness, water in the desert.

As we close this week, lift your eyes. What new thing might be springing up?

Sit With This:

What "former things" are you dwelling on? What keeps your eyes fixed on what was instead of what might be?

____

____

____

____

____

____

____

____

Look around. Do you perceive anything new springing up? Even small green shoots?

____

____

____

____

____

____

____

____

Week Six Reflection:

What has been uprooted this week? What are you beginning to see in the cleared ground?

____

____

____

____

____

____

____

____

____

____

____

____

____

Carry This Forward:

God, You are doing a new thing. Help me stop dwelling on the former things long enough to see it. Open my eyes to the way You are making in my wilderness.

AMEN.

Week Seven

Who Is With Me?

Day 45

> "Two are better than one, because they have a good return for their labor: If either of them falls down, one can help the other up. But pity anyone who falls and has no one to help them up."
>
> **Ecclesiastes 4:9-10 (NIV)**

We were not made to walk alone. This is not weakness; it is design.

In seasons of disruption, we discover who our people really are. Some step forward. Some step back. Some surprise us with their presence. Others surprise us with their absence.

This week, we map our community. Who is with you in this?

Sit With This:

Who has shown up for you since your "What?!" moment? Who has stepped forward?

____

____

____

____

____

Who has stepped back or disappeared? (No need to judge them. Let's just notice.)

____

____

____

____

____

Carry This Forward:

Lord, thank You for the people who have shown up. Help me grieve the ones who stepped back. Show me who You have placed in my life for this season.
AMEN.

Day 46

> "Wounds from a friend can be trusted, but an enemy
> multiplies kisses."
>
> **Proverbs 27:6 (NIV)**

Not all support looks the same. Some people comfort us. Others challenge us. Both are necessary.

Comforters sit with us in the pain. They do not try to fix. They hold space.

Challengers tell us hard truths. They see when we are stuck and love us enough to say so.

We need both in our circle. Too much comfort without challenge and we stay stuck. Too much challenge without comfort and we feel unsupported.

Who plays which role in your life?

Sit With This:

Who are your comforters—the people who sit with you without trying to fix?

____

____

____

____

Who are your challengers—the people who love you enough to tell hard truths?

____

____

____

____

Are you missing one type? How might you cultivate what is lacking?

____

____

____

____

Carry This Forward:

God, give me wisdom about my community. Help me receive comfort when I need it and challenge when I need it. Surround me with people who will help me grow.
AMEN.

Day 47

> "Carry each other's burdens, and in this way you will fulfill the law of Christ."
>
> **Galatians 6:2 (NIV)**

Burden-carrying is mutual. We are called to carry others' burdens, and we are called to let others carry ours.

Many of us are better at the first than the second. We help, serve, support, but we resist receiving. We do not want to be a burden. We do not want to appear weak.

But refusing to let others carry our burdens robs them of the chance to fulfill the law of Christ. It also keeps us isolated when we need connection most.

I can say this from experience. As a therapist, a divorced single mother to an autistic nonverbal child, an only daughter for my mother and an only child for my father, carrying burdens was a way I had learned to develop my value.

And this in itself was a trap.
If I was the one everyone could count on, I mattered. If I was the strong one, I had worth. If I never needed help, I was safe from disappointment.

Going through my "What?!" seasons created opportunities for me to reset this unrealistic expectation and truly learn the beauty of community, the wealth of connection and support. I could not carry it all alone. And when I finally let others in, I discovered that receiving is not weakness. It is obedience. It is trust. It is freedom.

Who have you let carry your burden in this season? Who have you kept at arm's length?

Sit With This:

Who have you allowed to carry your burden? How did it feel to let them help?

____

____

____

Who have you kept at arm's length? Why?

____

____

____

Is there someone you need to let in?

____

____

____

Carry This Forward:

Lord, help me receive help. Soften my resistance to being carried. Show me who I can let in.
AMEN.

Day 48

> "But Ruth replied, 'Don't urge me to leave you or to turn back from you. Where you go I will go, and where you stay I will stay. Your people will be my people and your God my God. Where you die I will die, and there I will be buried."
>
> **Ruth 1:16-17 (NIV)**

Ruth's commitment to Naomi is one of the most beautiful declarations of loyalty in Scripture. She chose to stay when she had every reason to leave.

In your life, who has made that choice? Who has stayed when leaving would have been easier?

And have you been that person for someone else? Even in your own disruption, have you stayed with someone?

Sit With This:

Who has "Ruthed" you? Who has stayed when they could have left, committed when they could have walked away?

____

____

____

____

____

____

Have you been able to "Ruth" anyone else, even in your own hard season?

____

____

____

____

____

____

Carry This Forward:

Lord, thank You for the people who have stayed. Help me be someone who stays for others. Grow my capacity for loyalty and commitment.
AMEN.

Day 49

> "Therefore encourage one another and build each other up, just as in fact you are doing."
>
> **1 Thessalonians 5:11 (NIV)**

Encouragement is not flattery. It is speaking truth about someone's value, potential, and God's presence in their life.

In hard seasons, we need people who encourage us and who remind us of what is true when we cannot see it ourselves.

We also need to be that voice for others. Even when we are struggling, we have something to offer.

Sit With This:

Who has encouraged you in this season? What did they say or do that built you up?

____

____

____

____

____

____

Who might need your encouragement right now? Even in your struggle, how might you build someone else up?

____

____

____

____

____

____

Carry This Forward:

God, thank You for the encouragers in my life. Make me an encourager too. Even in my struggle, let me build others up.
In Jesus' name,
AMEN.

Day 50

> "For where two or three gather in my name, there am I with them."
>
> **Matthew 18:20 (NIV)**

Community is not just about human connection. When we gather in Jesus' name, He is present.

This does not mean we need a formal church service. Two or three friends praying together. A small group meeting over coffee. A phone call where you invite God into the conversation.

Where are you experiencing Christ's presence through community?

Sit With This:

Where have you experienced Jesus showing up in community? When has gathering with others in His name felt especially meaningful?

____

____

____

____

____

____

If you have not experienced this recently, what is one step you could take toward it?

____

____

____

____

____

____

Carry This Forward:

*Jesus, show up when we gather. Be present in my community.
Help me seek You in the company of others.*
In Jesus' name,
AMEN.

Day 51

"And let us consider how we may spur one another on toward love and good deeds, not giving up meeting together, as some are in the habit of doing, but encouraging one another—and all the more as you see the Day approaching."

Hebrews 10:24-25 (NIV)

Meeting together matters. Not because we earn points for attendance, but because isolation is dangerous.

In hard seasons, we are tempted to withdraw. Church feels like too much. Small groups feel exhausting. Friends feel overwhelming.

I understand this tension personally. Due to my son's need to move, his sensory sensitivities, and his vocal stimming, sometimes connecting can be anxiety-provoking. I wonder how people will respond. I calculate whether the environment will work for him. I weigh whether the effort of showing up is worth the potential stress.

But even with all of that, it is still important for both him and me to have community. We need people. We need to be known. We need to belong somewhere, even if belonging looks different for us than it does for others.

Sometimes we do need solitude. But prolonged isolation usually makes things worse. As we close this week, assess your community engagement. Are you meeting with others, or have you withdrawn?

Sit With This:

Have you withdrawn from community in this season? If so, why?

____

____

____

____

What is one small step toward re-engagement? Not a giant leap—just one step.

____

____

____

____

Week Seven Reflection:

Draw a simple map of your community. Who is in your inner circle? Who is in the next ring out? Who are the acquaintances at the edge? What does this map reveal?

____

____

____

Carry This Forward:

Lord, keep me from isolation. Give me courage to show up, even when I am tired. Help me receive from community and contribute to it.
In Jesus' name,
AMEN.

Week Eight

What Does God Say About Me?

Day 52

> "For he chose us in him before the creation of the world to be holy and blameless in his sight. In love he predestined us for adoption to sonship through Jesus Christ, in accordance with his pleasure and will."
>
> **Ephesians 1:4-5 (NIV)**

Before the world existed, God chose you. Before your "What?!" moment. Before your successes or failures. Before anything you did or did not do.

You were chosen in love. Adopted as His child. This was not a backup plan, it was His pleasure and will.

This week, we anchor our identity in what God says about us. Not what circumstances say. Not what our failures say. Not what other people say. What God says.

Sit With This:

What does it mean to you that God chose you before the creation of the world? How does that truth interact with your current circumstances?

____

____

____

____

____

____

____

____

____

____

____

____

____

Carry This Forward:

Father, You chose me. Before I did anything to earn it or lose it. Help me live from that chosen ness, not toward it.

In Jesus' name,
AMEN.

Day 53

> "Therefore, if anyone is in Christ, the new creation has come: The old has gone, the new is here!"
>
> **2 Corinthians 5:17 (NIV)**

In Christ, you are new. Not improved but NEW. The old has gone. The new is here.

Your "What?!" moment may have changed your circumstances, your relationships, your plans. But it did not change your fundamental identity in Christ. You are still a new creation. That newness remains, even when everything else feels shattered.

Sit With This:

What parts of your identity feel shattered by your "What?!"
moment?

____

____

____

____

____

____

What parts of your identity in Christ remain untouched by
circumstances?

____

____

____

____

____

____

Carry This Forward:

_God, remind me that I am a new creation. What was true about
my identity in Christ before my "What?!" moment is still true
now. Help me live from that unchanging foundation._
In Jesus' name,
AMEN.

Day 54

> "The Lord your God is with you, the Mighty Warrior who saves. He will take great delight in you; in his love he will no longer rebuke you, but will rejoice over you with singing."
>
> **Zephaniah 3:17 (NIV)**

God delights in you. He rejoices over you with singing. Not because of what you produce.

Not because you have your life together. Not because you handled your "What?!" moment perfectly.

He delights in you because you are His.

Sit With This:

Do you believe God delights in you? Do you really believe it, not just intellectually assent to it?

____

____

____

____

____

____

What would change if you truly lived as someone God rejoices over with singing?

____

____

____

____

____

____

Carry This Forward:

Lord, help me receive Your delight. You are not disappointed in me. You rejoice over me with singing. Let that truth sink deep into my identity.
In Jesus' name,
AMEN.

Day 55

> "Therefore, there is now no condemnation for those who are in Christ Jesus."
>
> **Romans 8:1 (NIV)**

No condemnation. Not "reduced condemnation." Not "condemnation only for the big sins." None.

If you are in Christ, the verdict is in. You are not condemned.

This does not mean you will not face consequences. It does not mean you never make mistakes. It means the final word over your life is not guilty, but forgiven.

Whatever your "What?!" moment exposed, if there were failures or weaknesses came to light, there is no condemnation for you in Christ.

Sit With This:

What condemnation have you been carrying? What verdict have you pronounced over yourself?

____

____

____

____

____

____

How does Romans 8:1 speak to that self-condemnation?

____

____

____

____

____

____

____

Carry This Forward:

Jesus, there is no condemnation for me in You. Help me release the guilty verdicts I have pronounced over myself. I receive Your acquittal.
In Jesus' name,
AMEN.

Day 56

> "But you are a chosen people, a royal priesthood, a holy nation, God's special possession, that you may declare the praises of him who called you out of darkness into his wonderful light."
>
> **1 Peter 2:9 (NIV)**

Look at what God calls you: Chosen. Royal. Holy. His special possession.

These are not aspirational titles. They are current realities. Right now, in the middle of your "What?!" moment, you are royalty. You are holy. You are God's treasured possession.

Sit With This:

Which of these identity statements is hardest for you to believe right now? Chosen? Royal? Holy? Special possession?

____

____

____

____

____

____

____

What would change if you fully embraced that identity?

____

____

____

____

____

____

Carry This Forward:

Lord, I am chosen. I am royal. I am holy. I am Your special possession. Help me live from these truths, not toward them.
In Jesus' name,
AMEN.

Day 57

> "The Lord appeared to us in the past, saying: 'I have loved you with an everlasting love; I have drawn you with unfailing kindness."
>
> **Jeremiah 31:3 (NIV)**

God's love for you is everlasting. It does not expire. It does not fluctuate based on your performance. It does not diminish when you struggle.

He draws you with unfailing kindness. Not coercion. Not guilt. Kindness.

Sit With This:

Do you experience God's love as everlasting and kind? Or does it feel conditional and demanding?

____

____

____

____

____

____

What would it look like to be drawn by kindness rather than driven by guilt?

____

____

____

____

____

____

Carry This Forward:

Father, Your love is everlasting. Your kindness never fails. Draw me close with Your gentle love. I receive it today.
In Jesus' name,
AMEN.

Day 58

> "For you created my inmost being; you knit me together in my mother's womb. I praise you because I am fearfully and wonderfully made; your works are wonderful, I know that full well."
>
> **Psalm 139:13-14 (NIV)**

You are not an accident. You are not a mistake. You were knit together, carefully, intentionally, wonderfully.

Your "What?!" moment did not change how you were made. It did not erase the wonder of your creation. You remain fearfully and wonderfully made.

Sit With This:

Do you believe you are fearfully and wonderfully made? Does your "What?!" moment make that harder to believe?

____

____

____

____

What parts of how God made you are you grateful for?

____

____

____

____

Week Eight Reflection:

What has God been saying about your identity this week? Which truths have landed? Which do you still struggle to believe?

____

____

____

____

Carry This Forward:

Creator, You made me on purpose, with purpose. I am fearfully and wonderfully made. Help me know that full well, even in this season.

AMEN.

Day 59-60

Scripture Immersion

For the final two days of Part Two, we return to the practice of Scripture immersion. These twenty verses speak to identity, belonging, and God's declaration over our lives.

List of Scriptures on Identity

> "So God created mankind in his own image, in the image of God he created them; male and female he created them."
>
> **Genesis 1:27 (NIV)**

> "I praise you because I am fearfully and wonderfully made; your works are wonderful, I know that full well."
>
> **Psalm 139:14(NIV)**

> "But now, this is what the Lord says—he who created you, Jacob, he who formed you, Israel: "Do not fear, for I have redeemed you; I have summoned you by name; you are mine."
>
> **Isaiah 43:1 (NIV)**

> "This is what the Lord says—he who made you, who formed you in the womb, and who will help you: Do not be afraid, Jacob, my servant, Jeshurun, whom I have chosen."
>
> **Isaiah 44:2 (NIV)**

"You will be a crown of splendor in the Lord's hand, a royal diadem in the hand of your God. No longer will they call you Deserted, or name your land Desolate. But you will be called Hephzibah, and your land Beulah; for the Lord will take delight in you."

Isaiah 62:3-4 (NIV)

"Before I formed you in the womb I knew you, before you were born I set you apart; I appointed you as a prophet to the nations."

Jeremiah 1:5 (NIV)

"You are the light of the world. A town built on a hill cannot be hidden."

Matthew 5:14 (NIV)

"Yet to all who did receive him, to those who believed in his name, he gave the right to become children of God."

John 1:12 (NIV)

"I no longer call you servants, because a servant does not know his master's business. Instead, I have called you friends, for everything that I learned from my Father I have made known to you."

John 15:15 (NIV)

"The Spirit you received does not make you slaves, so that you live in fear again; rather, the Spirit you received brought about your adoption to sonship. And by him we cry, "Abba, Father." The Spirit himself testifies with our spirit that we are God's children."

Romans 8:15-16 (NIV)

"No, in all these things we are more than conquerors through him who loved us."

Romans 8:37 (NIV)

"Do you not know that your bodies are temples of the Holy Spirit, who is in you, whom you have received from God? You are not your own; you were bought at a price. Therefore honor God with your bodies."

1 Corinthians 6:19-20 (NIV)

"Therefore, if anyone is in Christ, the new creation has come: The old has gone, the new is here!"

2 Corinthians 5:17 (NIV)

"We are therefore Christ's ambassadors, as though God were making his appeal through us."

2 Corinthians 5:20 (NIV)

"So in Christ Jesus you are all children of God through faith"

Galatians 3:26 (NIV)

"For we are God's handiwork, created in Christ Jesus to do good works, which God prepared in advance for us to do."

Ephesians 2:10 (NIV)

"For you died, and your life is now hidden with Christ in God."

Colossians 3:3 (NIV)

"But you are a chosen people, a royal priesthood, a holy nation, God's special possession, that you may declare the praises of him who called you out of darkness into his wonderful light."

1 Peter 2:9 (NIV)

"See what great love the Father has lavished on us, that we should be called children of God! And that is what we are!"

1 John 3:1 (NIV)

"And has made us to be a kingdom and priests to serve his God and Father—to him be glory and power for ever and ever! "
AMEN.

Revelation 1:6 (NIV)

Day 59

Read and Receive

Read through all twenty scriptures slowly. Notice which ones resonate.

Which three scriptures spoke most directly to your identity today?

1. ____

____

2. ____

____

3. ____

____

What do they stir in you?

____

____

____

____

____

____

Carry This Forward:

Lord, Your Word tells me who I am. Let these identity truths take root in me.
In Jesus' name,
AMEN.

Day 30

Return and Reflect

Write out the three scriptures that spoke to you:

Scripture 1:

____

____

____

____

Scripture 2:

____

____

____

____

____

Scripture 3:

____

____

____

____

____

Part Two: Reflection

You have completed Part Two. You have examined what you believed before, what is being uprooted, who is with you, and what God says about your identity.

What surprised you in this part? What shifted? What still needs tending?

____

____

____

____

____

What is one truth you want to carry into Part Three?

____

____

____

____

____

Carry This Forward:

Father, I have attended to what You are revealing in me. I have examined my roots. I have mapped my community. I have anchored my identity in what You say about me. As I move into the final thirty days, prepare me for growth.
In Jesus' name,
AMEN.

Part Three: Allign

Days 61-90

"He who began a good work in you will carry it on to completion." Philippians 1:6

You have done the work of acknowledgment. You have attended to what was being revealed. Now it is time to align and orient yourself toward what comes next.

Part Three is not about pretending the "What?!" moment did not happen. It is about integrating it. Taking everything you have learned, grieved, and discovered, and asking: How do I move forward from here?

This is not rushing toward resolution. It is taking faithful next steps. It is asking what remains true even after everything has changed. It is imagining what new fruit might grow from roots that have been tended.

You are not the same person you were ninety days ago. You have been through something. And God is not finished with you yet.

Let us align with what He is doing.

Week Nine

What Is Still True?

Day 61

> "I the Lord do not change."
>
> **Malachi 3:6 (NIV)**

Everything around you may have changed. But God has not. His character is the same.

His love is the same. His promises are the same. His presence is the same.

This is not just theological information, it is a handhold in the chaos. When everything shifts, we need something immovable to grip. God is that immovable thing.

This week, we anchor to what remains true even after everything has changed.

Sit With This:

What feels like it has changed about everything? List the shifts both, internal and external.

____

____

____

____

____

____

Now list what has not changed about God. What remains true about His character?

____

____

____

____

____

____

Carry This Forward:

*Lord, You do not change. When everything around me shifts,
You remain. Help me grip Your unchanging nature as my
anchor.*
AMEN.

Day 62

"Jesus Christ is the same yesterday and today and forever."

Hebrews 13:8 (NIV)

Yesterday—before your "What?!" moment—Jesus was faithful.

Today—in the middle of the chaos—Jesus is faithful.

Forever—no matter what comes—Jesus will be faithful.

His consistency is not passive; it is active. He is actively the same. Actively loving. Actively present. Actively working.

Sit With This:

How did you experience Jesus before your "What?!" moment?

____

____

____

____

How are you experiencing Him now, in the middle of it?

____

____

____

____

What do you hope to experience from Him in the future?

____

____

____

____

Carry This Forward:

Jesus, You are the same yesterday, today, and forever. Your faithfulness does not waver. Help me trust Your consistency.
In Jesus' name,
AMEN.

Day 63

> "Your word, Lord, is eternal; it stands firm in the heavens.
> Your faithfulness continues through all generations."
> **Psalm 119:89-90 (NIV)**

God's Word stands firm. It does not bend to circumstances. It does not weaken with time. It is eternal.

The promises you read in Scripture before your "What?!" moment are still valid. The truths you memorized still apply. The Word remains.

Sit With This:

What Scripture truths have anchored you in this season?

____

____

____

____

____

____

What promise from God's Word do you most need to hold onto right now?

____

____

____

____

____

____

Carry This Forward:

Lord, Your Word stands firm. It does not change with my circumstances. Help me build my life on what remains true forever.
In Jesus' name,
AMEN.

Day 64

> "For no one is cast off by the Lord forever. Though he brings grief, he will show compassion, so great is his unfailing love. For he does not willingly bring affliction or grief to the children of mankind."
>
> **Lamentations 3:31-33 (NIV)**

God does not delight in your pain. He does not willingly afflict. When grief comes, it is not because He wanted you to hurt.

And even in the grief, compassion is coming. Not might come but WILL come. His unfailing love guarantees it.

Sit With This:

Have you felt cast off in this season? What would it mean to believe that this is not permanent?

____

____

____

____

____

____

Where have you seen glimpses of compassion breaking through?

____

____

____

____

____

____

Carry This Forward:

Father, You do not willingly afflict. Compassion is coming. Help me hold onto that promise when the grief feels endless.
In Jesus' name,
AMEN.

Day 65

> "God is not human, that he should lie, not a human being, that he should change his mind. Does he speak and then not act? Does he promise and not fulfill?"
>
> **Numbers 23:19 (NIV)**

God keeps His promises. Every single one.

Some promises have conditions we do not fully understand. Some operate on timelines we cannot see. But God does not make empty commitments. What He has spoken, He will do.

Sit With This:

What promises from God are you waiting to see fulfilled?

____

____

____

____

____

____

____

What helps you trust His timing when fulfillment seems delayed?

____

____

____

____

____

____

____

Carry This Forward:

Lord, You are not a liar. What You have promised, You will fulfill. Help me trust Your timing even when I cannot see the way forward.
In Jesus' name,
AMEN.

Day 66

"The grass withers and the flowers fall, but the word of our God endures forever."

Isaiah 40:8 (NIV)

Everything temporary will pass. Circumstances change. Feelings shift. Relationships evolve. Bodies age.

But God's Word endures. What He has spoken over your life is not subject to decay.

Sit With This:

What temporary things have you been gripping too tightly?

____

____

____

____

____

____

What eternal truths can you hold onto instead?

____

____

____

____

____

____

Carry This Forward:

God, help me hold temporary things loosely and eternal things tightly. Your Word endures. Let me build on what lasts.
In Jesus' name,
AMEN.

Day 67

> "And we know that in all things God works for the good of those who love him, who have been called according to his purpose."
>
> **Romans 8:28 (NIV)**

We return to this verse with new eyes. Sixty-seven days in, you have context you did not have at the start. You have named your pain, attended to your roots, and begun to see what remains true.

Now you can receive this promise differently. Not as a dismissal of pain, but as a statement of trust. God is working. In all things. For good.

Sit With This:

How has your understanding of Romans 8:28 deepened over these sixty-seven days?

____

____

____

What "good" are you beginning to glimpse or hoping to see?

____

____

____

Week Nine Reflection:

What remains true that you can anchor to? What unchanging realities will you grip as you move forward?

____

____

____

Carry This Forward:

Father, You are working for good. I trust You. Even what I cannot see, I trust You.

In Jesus' name,

AMEN.

Week Ten

What New Thing Is Possible?

Day 68

God specializes in new things. He makes ways where there are none. He brings water to deserts.

When I felt the most deserted was after being sexually assaulted in my apartment by a maintenance worker while my son was home.

I left that unit, and with the help of close friends and my family, I drove my son and our belongings over 500 miles back to my hometown. I felt out of my body and out of my mind. I was returning to the very place I had been running from after my divorce.

However, even in the midst of that moment, I recognize now that God was creating something new for me and my son. My hometown became the place of community, connection, and autism supports that my son could not have received in the city we left. What felt like retreat was actually restoration. What felt like failure was actually redirection.

When something is drying up, something somewhere else will spring up. Believe that.

Your "What?!" moment may have felt like the end. But God is in the business of new beginnings. What new thing might be springing up?

Sit With This:

Where do you see even the smallest evidence of something new beginning?

____

____

____

____

____

____

____

What new thing would you like to see God do in your life?

____

____

____

____

____

____

____

Carry This Forward:

Lord, You are doing a new thing. Open my eyes to perceive it. Make a way in my wilderness. Bring streams to my wasteland.
In Jesus' name,
AMEN.

Day 69

> "He who was seated on the throne said, 'I am making all things new!' Then he said, 'Write this down, for these words are trustworthy and true."
>
> **Revelation 21:5 (NIV)**

All things. Not some things. All things.

This is the ultimate promise, that everything broken will be made new. Not just patched. Not just improved. New.

Your "What?!" moment is not outside the scope of God's redemptive work.

Sit With This:

What feels too broken to be made new?

____

____

____

____

____

____

What would it look like for God to make that thing new?

____

____

____

____

____

____

Carry This Forward:

*God, You are making all things new. Even the things that feel
beyond repair. I trust Your redemptive work.*
In Jesus' name,
AMEN.

Day 70

> "For I know the plans I have for you," declares the Lord, plans to prosper you and not to harm you, plans to give you hope and a future."
>
> **Jeremiah 29:11 (NIV)**

God has plans for you. After the "What?!" moment. After the grief. After the upheaval. There are still plans.

These plans are not harm. They are hope. They are future.

Sit With This:

What fears do you have about your future?

____

____

____

____

____

____

What hopes are beginning to emerge?

____

____

____

____

____

____

Carry This Forward:

Lord, You have plans for me. Plans for hope and a future. Help me trust that my story is not over.

In Jesus' name,
AMEN.

Day 71

> "Now to him who is able to do immeasurably more than all we ask or imagine, according to his power that is at work within us."

Ephesians 3:20 (NIV)

Immeasurably more. Beyond what we ask. Beyond what we imagine.

Our vision is limited. Our dreams are constrained by what we have seen and experienced. But God operates beyond our imagination.

What might He be planning that you have not even thought to ask for?

Sit With This:

What have you been asking God for?

____

____

____

____

____

____

What might be "immeasurably more" than what you are
asking?

____

____

____

____

____

Carry This Forward:

*Father, You can do more than I ask or imagine. Expand my
vision. Work according to Your power, not my limited
expectations.*
In Jesus' name,
AMEN.

Day 72

> "Therefore, if anyone is in Christ, the new creation has come: The old has gone, the new is here!"
>
> **2 Corinthians 5:17 (NIV)**

You are already new in Christ. This is not something you are becoming, it is something you already are.

From this newness, anything is possible. Your history does not define your future. Your "What?!" moment does not have the final word.

Sit With This:

What parts of your "old self" are you ready to release?

____

____

____

____

____

____

____

What aspects of your "new self" are you ready to embrace?

____

____

____

____

____

____

____

Carry This Forward:

Lord, I am a new creation. The old has gone. Help me live from my newness, not my history.
In Jesus' name,
AMEN.

Day 73

> "Brothers and sisters, I do not consider myself yet to have taken hold of it. But one thing I do: Forgetting what is behind and straining toward what is ahead, I press on toward the goal to win the prize for which God has called me heavenward in Christ Jesus."
>
> **Philippians 3:13-14 (NIV)**

Paul was not paralyzed by his past. He had plenty to regret, he persecuted Christians. But he chose to forget what was behind and strain toward what was ahead.

This does not mean denying history. It means not letting it anchor you. You can acknowledge what happened and still press forward.

Sit With This:

What are you having trouble leaving behind?

____

____

____

____

____

____

What would "straining toward what is ahead" look like for you?

____

____

____

____

____

____

Carry This Forward:

God, help me press on. Not denying my past, but not being imprisoned by it. I strain toward what is ahead.
In Jesus' name,
AMEN.

Day 74

"Yet this I call to mind and therefore I have hope: Because of the Lord's great love we are not consumed, though his compassions never fail. They are new every morning; great is your faithfulness."

Lamentations 3:21-23 (NIV)

New mercies every morning. Not recycled. Not leftover. Fresh.

Tomorrow, when you wake up, there will be new compassion waiting for you. You do not have to manufacture it. You just have to receive it.

Sit With This:

What new mercy do you need for tomorrow?

____

____

____

____

How can you position yourself to receive it?

____

____

____

____

Week Ten Reflection:

What new things are you beginning to see as possible? What hope is emerging?

____

____

____

____

Carry This Forward:

Lord, Your compassions are new every morning. Great is Your faithfulness. I receive tomorrow's mercy in advance.

In Jesus' name,

AMEN.

Week Eleven

Who Am I Becoming?

Day 75

> "For those God foreknew he also predestined to be conformed to the image of his Son, that he might be the firstborn among many brothers and sisters."
>
> **Romans 8:29 (NIV)**

You are being conformed to the image of Christ. This is the destination of your transformation. Not just a better version of yourself, but an image-bearer of Jesus.

Your "What?!" moment is part of this conforming process. Not the whole picture, but part of it.

Sit With This:

How have you grown more Christlike through this season?

____

____

____

____

____

____

What Christlike qualities do you want to see developed
further?

____

____

____

____

____

____

Carry This Forward:

*Lord, conform me to the image of Your Son. Use everything,
even this, to make me more like Jesus.*

In Jesus' name,
AMEN.

Day 76

> "But the fruit of the Spirit is love, joy, peace, forbearance, kindness, goodness, faithfulness, gentleness and self-control. Against such things there is no law."
>
> **Galatians 5:22-23 (NIV)**

The fruit of the Spirit is what grows when we are connected to the Vine. It is not manufactured through effort, it is cultivated through relationship.

Which characteristic of the fruit is developing in you through this season?

Sit With This:

Which characteristic of the fruit of the Spirit have you seen growing in this season?

____

____

____

____

____

____

Which ones are still lacking? How might you cultivate them?

____

____

____

____

____

____

____

Carry This Forward:

Holy Spirit, produce Your fruit in
In Jesus' name,
AMEN.

Day 77

"But by the grace of God I am what I am, and his grace to me was not without effect. No, I worked harder than all of them—yet not I, but the grace of God that was with me."

1 Corinthians 15:10 (NIV)

By grace, you are what you are. Not by your effort alone. Not by your willpower. By grace.

And yet grace is not passive. Paul worked hard. But even his work was empowered by grace.

Who are you becoming by the grace of God?

Sit With This:

How has grace shaped who you are becoming?

____

____

____

____

____

____

Where do you see grace empowering your work and growth?

____

____

____

____

____

____

Carry This Forward:

Lord, by Your grace I am what I am. May Your grace not be without effect in my life. Empower my work and growth.
In Jesus' name,
AMEN.

Day 78

> "And we all, who with unveiled faces contemplate the Lord's glory, are being transformed into his image with ever-increasing glory, which comes from the Lord, who is the Spirit."
>
> **2 Corinthians 3:18 (NIV)**

Transformation happens as we contemplate God's glory. The more we look at Him, the more we become like Him.

This is gradual "ever-increasing glory." Not instant, but progressive.

Sit With This:

How are you contemplating God's glory in this season? What practices keep your face unveiled before Him?

____

____

____

____

____

____

Where do you see transformation happening, even slowly?

____

____

____

____

____

____

Carry This Forward:

Lord, I want to contemplate Your glory. Transform me into Your image with ever-increasing glory. Keep my face unveiled before you.
In Jesus' name,
AMEN.

Day 79

> "You were taught, with regard to your former way of life, to put off your old self, which is being corrupted by its deceitful desires; to be made new in the attitude of your minds; and to put on the new self, created to be like God in true righteousness and holiness."
>
> **Ephesians 4:22-24 (NIV)**

Put off the old. Put on the new. This is an intentional action to choose who we will be.

Your "What?!" moment may have stripped away some of the old without your permission. Now you get to choose what you put on.

Sit With This:

What parts of your "old self" has this season helped you put off?

____

____

____

____

____

____

What aspects of your "new self" are you choosing to put on?

____

____

____

____

____

____

____

Carry This Forward:

God, I put off the old. I put on the new. Renew the attitude of my mind. Create in me true righteousness and holiness.
In Jesus' name,
AMEN.

Day 80

"Therefore, as God's chosen people, holy and dearly loved, clothe yourselves with compassion, kindness, humility, gentleness and patience. Bear with each other and forgive one another if any of you has a grievance against someone. Forgive as the Lord forgave you. And over all these virtues put on love, which binds them all together in perfect unity."

Colossians 3:12-14 (NIV)

Clothe yourself with compassion, kindness, humility, gentleness, patience. Put on love over all.

This is who you are becoming: someone dressed in virtue, bound together by love.

Sit With This:

Which of these "clothes" do you need to put on more
intentionally?

____

____

____

____

____

____

Is there forgiveness you need to extend—to others or
yourself?

____

____

____

____

____

____

Carry This Forward:

*Lord, clothe me with compassion, kindness, humility,
gentleness, and patience. Put on me Your love that binds
everything together.*
In Jesus' name,
AMEN.

Day 81

> "In all this you greatly rejoice, though now for a little while you may have had to suffer grief in all kinds of trials. These have come so that the proven genuineness of your faith—of greater worth than gold, which perishes even though refined by fire—may result in praise, glory and honor when Jesus Christ is revealed."
>
> **1 Peter 1:6-7 (NIV)**

Your faith is being refined. The fire does not feel good, but it produces something precious: proven, genuine faith.

This faith is worth more than gold. And when Jesus is revealed, it will result in praise, glory, and honor.

Sit With This:

How has your faith been refined through this season?

____

____

____

____

What is the "proven genuineness" that is emerging?

____

____

____

Week Eleven Reflection:

Who are you becoming? What identity is emerging from the ashes of your "What?!" moment?

____

____

____

Carry This Forward:

Lord, refine my faith. Let it be proven genuine. May it result in praise and glory and honor to You.
In Jesus' name,
AMEN.

Week Twelve

What Fruit Will I Cultivate?

Day 82

> "I am the vine; you are the branches. If you remain in me and I in you, you will bear much fruit; apart from me you can do nothing."
>
> **John 15:5 (NIV)**

Fruit is the natural result of connection. Branches do not strain to produce grapes however they receive life from the vine, and fruit follows.

Your "What?!" moment may have taught you how little you can do apart from Christ. Now, as you move forward, let that dependence remain.

Sit With This:

What has this season taught you about your dependence on Christ?

____

____

____

____

____

____

How can you remain connected to the Vine as you move forward?

____

____

____

____

____

____

Carry This Forward:

Jesus, You are the Vine. I am the branch. Help me remain in You. Apart from You, I can do nothing. In You, I will bear much fruit.
In Jesus' name,
AMEN.

Day 83

> "Likewise, every good tree bears good fruit, but a bad tree bears bad fruit. A good tree cannot bear bad fruit, and a bad tree cannot bear good fruit."
>
> **Matthew 7:17-18 (NIV)**

The fruit reveals the root. What grows from you shows what is planted in you.

Over ninety days, you have tended your roots by acknowledging what happened, attending to what was revealed, and aligning with God's work. What fruit do you want to see from this tending?

Sit With This:

What kind of fruit do you want your life to produce going forward?

____

____

____

____

____

____

What seeds have been planted that will make this fruit possible?

____

____

____

____

____

____

Carry This Forward:

Lord, let me be a good tree bearing good fruit. May what grows from my life reveal roots planted deep in You.
In Jesus' name,
AMEN.

Day 84

> "Blessed is the one who does not walk in step with the wicked or stand in the way that sinners take or sit in the company of mockers, but whose delight is in the law of the Lord, and who meditates on his law day and night. That person is like a tree planted by streams of water, which yields its fruit in season and whose leaf does not wither—whatever they do prospers."
>
> **Psalm 1:1-3 (NIV)**

Trees planted by water yield fruit in season. Not every season but in season. There is rhythm to fruitfulness.

Your "What?!" moment may have disrupted your rhythm. As you move forward, what season are you entering? What fruit is appropriate for this season?

Sit With This:

What season are you entering now?

____

____

____

____

____

____

What fruit is appropriate to cultivate in this season?

____

____

____

____

____

____

____

Carry This Forward:

Lord, plant me by streams of water. Let me yield fruit in season.
May my leaf not wither.
In Jesus' name,
AMEN.

Day 85

> "So that you may live a life worthy of the Lord and please him in every way: bearing fruit in every good work, growing in the knowledge of God."
>
> **Colossians 1:10 (NIV)**

Fruit is not just about internal character. It is also about good works, the actions that flow from a transformed life.

As you leave these ninety days, what good works is God calling you to?

Sit With This:

What good works do you feel called to pursue?

____

____

____

____

____

____

How has your "What?!" moment prepared you for these works?

____

____

____

____

____

____

Carry This Forward:

Lord, help me bear fruit in every good work. Grow me in knowledge of You. Let my life be worthy of Your name.
In Jesus' name,
AMEN.

Day 87

> "Let us not become weary in doing good, for at the proper time we will reap a harvest if we do not give up."
>
> **Galatians 6:9 (NIV)**

Harvest comes at the proper time, not immediately, and not on our schedule. The key is not giving up.

Ninety days is a significant journey. But it is not the end. Keep doing good. Keep tending roots. Keep cultivating fruit.

Sit With This:

Where are you tempted to give up?

____

____

____

____

____

____

What will help you persevere until harvest?

____

____

____

____

____

____

Carry This Forward:

Lord, help me not become weary. At the proper time, I will reap if I do not give up. Sustain me.
In Jesus' name,
AMEN.

Day 88

> "Sow righteousness for yourselves, reap the fruit of unfailing love, and break up your unplowed ground; for it is time to seek the Lord, until he comes and showers his righteousness on you."
>
> **Hosea 10:12 (NIV)**

Break up the unplowed ground. This is the hard work of preparation, turning soil that has been compacted, making it ready for seed.

Your "What?!" moment broke up some ground. Now you get to choose what you sow.

Sit With This:

What ground has been broken up in you?

____

____

____

____

What righteousness will you sow there?

____

____

____

____

Week Twelve Reflection:

What fruit will you cultivate going forward? What harvest do you hope to see?

____

____

____

____

Carry This Forward:

Lord, I sow righteousness. I break up unplowed ground. Shower Your righteousness on me. Let me reap the fruit of unfailing love.
AMEN.

Day 89-90

Final Scripture Immersion and Commissioning

Day 89: List of Scriptures on Moving Forward

Read through these verses about hope, purpose, and future. Highlight the ones that will carry you forward.

> "Trust in the Lord with all your heart and lean not on your own understanding; in all your ways submit to him, and he will make your paths straight."
>
> **Proverbs 3:5-6 (NIV)**

> "But those who hope in the Lord will renew their strength. They will soar on wings like eagles; they will run and not grow weary, they will walk and not be faint."
>
> **Isaiah 40:31 (NIV)**

> "So do not fear, for I am with you; do not be dismayed, for I am your God. I will strengthen you and help you; I will uphold you with my righteous right hand."
>
> **Isaiah 41:10 (NIV)**

"Forget the former things; do not dwell on the past. See, I am doing a new thing! Now it springs up; do you not perceive it? I am making a way in the wilderness and streams in the wasteland."

Isaiah 43:18-19 (NIV)

"So is my word that goes out from my mouth: It will not return to me empty, but will accomplish what I desire and achieve the purpose for which I sent it."

Isaiah 55:11 (NIV)

"For I know the plans I have for you," declares the Lord, "plans to prosper you and not to harm you, plans to give you hope and a future."

Jeremiah 29:11 (NIV)

"But as for me, I watch in hope for the Lord, I wait for God my Savior; my God will hear me."

Micah 7:7 (NIV)

"And we know that in all things God works for the good of those who love him, who have been called according to his purpose."

Romans 8:28 (NIV)

"May the God of hope fill you with all joy and peace as you trust in him, so that you may overflow with hope by the power of the Holy Spirit."

Romans 15:13 (NIV)

"Therefore we do not lose heart. Though outwardly we are wasting away, yet inwardly we are being renewed day by day. For our light and momentary troubles are producing for us an eternal glory that far outweighs them all. So we fix our eyes not on what is seen, but on what is unseen, since what is seen is temporary, but what is unseen is eternal."

2 Corinthians 4:16-18 (NIV)

"For we live by faith, not by sight."

2 Corinthians 5:7 (NIV)

"Being confident of this, that he who began a good work in you will carry it on to completion until the day of Christ Jesus."

Philippians 1:6 (NIV)

"Brothers and sisters, I do not consider myself yet to have taken hold of it. But one thing I do: Forgetting what is behind and straining toward what is ahead, I press on toward the goal to win the prize for which God has called me heavenward in Christ Jesus."

Philippians 3:13-14 (NIV)

"I can do all this through him who gives me strength."
Philippians 4:13 (NIV)

"Set your minds on things above, not on earthly things."
Colossians 3:2 (NIV)

"So do not throw away your confidence; it will be richly rewarded. You need to persevere so that when you have done the will of God, you will receive what he has promised."
Hebrews 10:35-36 (NIV)

"Therefore, since we are surrounded by such a great cloud of witnesses, let us throw off everything that hinders and the sin that so easily entangles. And let us run with perseverance the race marked out for us, fixing our eyes on Jesus, the pioneer and perfecter of faith."
Hebrews 12:12 (NIV)

"Consider it pure joy, my brothers and sisters, whenever you face trials of many kinds, because you know that the testing of your faith produces perseverance. Let perseverance finish its work so that you may be mature and complete, not lacking anything."

James 1:2-4 (NIV)

"And the God of all grace, who called you to his eternal glory in Christ, after you have suffered a little while, will himself restore you and make you strong, firm and steadfast."

1 Peter 5:10 (NIV)

"He who was seated on the throne said, "I am making all things new!" Then he said, "Write this down, for these words are trustworthy and true."

Revelation 21:5 (NIV)

Which three scriptures spoke most directly to your identity today?

1. ____

____

2. ____

____

3. ____

____

Write them out:

____

____

____

____

____

____

____

____

____

____

____

____

____

____

Day 90

Commissioning

You have done it. Ninety days of sacred work.

You acknowledged what happened. You attended to what was being revealed. You aligned with what God is doing.

You are not the same person who opened this devotional. You have been through something and you have been formed by it.

This is not the end. It is a new beginning. The roots you have tended will bear fruit. The truths you have anchored to will hold. The identity you have claimed will sustain you.

Final Reflection

Look back at your journey. What has changed in you?

What truths will you carry forward?

Who has God revealed Himself to be through this season?

Who are you now?

A Blessing for the Journey Ahead

May the God who sees you continue to see you.

May the Father who loves you continue to love you.

May the Spirit who comforts you continue to comfort you.

May the Savior who redeems you continue to redeem you. Go forward in peace.

Go forward in hope. Go forward in faith.

The "What?!" moment was not the end of your story. It was the beginning of something new.

You are seen. You are known. You are loved. You are His.

____

____

____

____

Carry This Forward:

Father, I have completed this journey, but I know You are not finished with me. He who began a good work will carry it on to completion. I march forward trusting You. Thank You for meeting me in my "What?!" moment. Thank You for not leaving me there. I am Yours forever
In Jesus' name,
AMEN.

About the Author

Tiana "Tee" Townsend, LMFT, is a Licensed Marriage and Family Therapist, Amazon bestselling author, and founder of Wiselign Consulting, LLC. With over a decade of clinical experience, she specializes in helping individuals and organizations navigate life's most challenging transitions.

Tiana's personal journey as a divorced single mother of a nonverbal autistic son has shaped her understanding of what it means to trust God in the "What?!" moments. Through her own seasons of upheaval—divorce, her son's diagnosis, trauma, and unexpected redirection—she has learned that the roots we tend determine the fruit we grow.

She is the author of the "A Seat on the Couch" urban fiction series, a relationship columnist for Speak Up Sis Magazine, and an active member of her church community where she serves in music ministry and youth leadership.

Tiana lives in California with her son, True. She believes no one should have to navigate life's hardest moments alone.

Connect with Tiana: www.iamtianatee.com
Instagram: @iamtianatee LinkedIn: @iamtianatee